COMMUNION

By
Walter Greason

Bloomington, IN Milton Keynes, UK

authorHOUSE®

AuthorHouse™
1663 Liberty Drive, Suite 200
Bloomington, IN 47403
www.authorhouse.com
Phone: 1-800-839-8640

AuthorHouse™ UK Ltd.
500 Avebury Boulevard
Central Milton Keynes, MK9 2BE
www.authorhouse.co.uk
Phone: 08001974150

This book is a work of fiction. People, places, events, and situations are the product of the author's imagination. Any resemblance to actual persons, living or dead, or historical events, is purely coincidental.

First published by AuthorHouse 3/5/2007

ISBN: 978-1-4259-5657-8 (sc)

Library of Congress Control Number: 2006907840

Printed in the United States of America
Bloomington, Indiana

This book is printed on acid-free paper.

ENDINGS

11th Lunar Cycle, 2050
Dehra Dun, India

Squeezing

Pushing

tightly

hard
pulling   screaming   forcing   struggling

into the light.

Sliding forward . . .
Where am I going?

What's happening to me?
Voices calling. . .

Shouts
insisting   demanding
my presence.

Surrounding and piercing every pore, a plaintiff wail --

at once, from both inside
and outside,
I try to
mimic the sound.

nothing happens . . .
and I try again . . .
but something

squeezes my
throat   . . .
tighter
and
tighter

What is it?

I turn my head
the shouting is louder
the screaming more shrill
tighter
and
tighter

I can't move my head

3

the light is getting brighter

                                                            I'm almost there

                                    tighter
                                    and

                                        I
                                        can't
                                        breathe . . .

*   *   *

My knuckles bared a rosy pink as I gripped the side rails.

        Sweat poured down my face and the wet black hair was splayed all over my head. I felt Anita turn inside me, and the doctor told me to "PUSH!"   If only he know how much this hurt . . .

                                        typical man.

"AWWW!"

        My screams . . .   OOOHHH!   Just for my baby to be born. My husband's arms held me, but, for all his good intentions, I wish he had stayed in the lobby. I grit my teeth.

"GRRRR."

        Anita was helping me . . . she wanted to come out -- God Bless Her! Each contracting push felt like it might tear me in half.

        The nurse moved to inject a pain killer into my IV.

                                                "NO!"

        I had to feel my baby! She stepped away quickly--and the doctor looked up at me in amazement . . . he shakes his head disbelieving as he insisted again ... "PUSH!"

                        So   I
                                    did . . .
                                            "Uhhhhh....."

        That's when I felt something go wrong. Anita should have been crying, her head was outside of me . . . I screamed, and tried to look down between my legs . .
.

                "What's Happening?!?"

        The doctor stayed down, head bowed in concentration and I felt his fingers trying to coax Anita out of me. My husband, tears welling in his eyes, gripped me tightly as I turned towards him. I began to feel lightheaded . . .

                                        dizzy.

The doctor's shouted words--I didn't understand them for some reason-- caused a great stir among the nurses, and I saw my blood all over his hands and face. Suddenly, exhaustion overwhelmed me . . . I was so tired . . . I just couldn't keep my eyes open.

Salman took my face in his hands and pleaded with me through his eyes. His mouth moved but there were no words. All I knew was I had to sleep. The pain no longer stabbed through my pelvis and the world darkened fuzzily around the edges. My hands slipped off of the rails, and the lights shone brightly in my eyes . . . I had to close my eyes. Salman's face became panicked, he gripped me and shook me -- his embrace was so insistent. But then I knew . . . I understood.

Eyes closed, I whispered to Salman, "Save Anita." Then even my voice failed me. The bright light strobed brilliantly . . . dazzling as it closed on me.   I believe I smiled ... until . . . the doctor's voice rose amidst a nauseating silence.

"I'm sorry. They're both gone."

Louder than even my husband's grieving sobs, my agonized, silent scream.

*   *   *

I dashed out of the room, through meaningless corridors, and into the cutting night wind . . . no more than five strides before I collapsed,
                    pain tearing streaks down both sides of my face.

My voice choked -- I could not even breathe their names,
                    I had betrayed their trust and their love.
          Somewhere deep inside, I crumbled . . . broken and defeated . . .
               my body fell flat to the cold dirt, and I wished . . .

I wished that my noisy inhalations would forever cease.

                                    .

                                    .

                                    .

          How much time has passed?
                         It didn't matter . . .
               in the next instant, the pain knotted my stomach
                                    and my failure saddled me again.

The blanket someone had wrapped around me provided no warmth. Stripped of my love, my pride, my joy, my hope . . .
                    nothing remained in me other than a cold gray, numbing despair,
                         and the torture of life after death.

I found my way to the morgue. (One lost her blood and died of shock.)

My mind told me--perhaps this was a dream? (The other strangled by her umbilical
                                                                                                cord.)
                        --a horrific nightmare . . .
            but Reema's frozen features told me otherwise.

                        Running my hand down her face, tears again flowed from
                                    my eyes.
She was so beautiful
            so strong . . .   I slid the shelf closed again, stumbling backwards
                        at the immutable reality of my failure.
Finding my baby's temporary resting place, paralysis locked my joints.
                        Deep down,
            I knew I could not face the child whose life I both created and destroyed.
                                                Yet something willed me forward.

"NO!"   "NO!"   "NO! NO! NO!"

Rage and shock dropped me to my knees, trembling and gasping for air.
On my daughter's, sweet Anita's,   shelf . . . there was
                                                                        nothing.
            I accosted the coroner for an explanation first,
                                                then my doctor,
                        then any doctor,
                                    then anyone,
            then everyone.

No one knew anything. My daughter was just gone.
No one knew what happened. Anita was now doubly lost to me.

The insanity of it all suffocated me.
            They sent a counselor to speak to me. Her transparent, hollow words were
as meaningless as my life --   then, I realized   . . .   I had to leave.

She protested, chasing me into the parking lot. The snow had just begun to fall-
-a soft, white corruption; a beauty whose lies dishonored my wife and daughter.
It didn't matter either. My purpose would not be dissuaded. I had direction and
meaning again. My family would be reunited.
                                                I would reunite us.

            Speeding northeast from Dehra Dun, I pressed the accelerator to the floor.
Cars on both sides of the road swerved to avoid my dark, determined charge.
The road was mine. I would be whole again! The engine whined against the
strain I placed upon it. The wheels shrieked in protest as I conquered the winding
mountain road.
I turned off my headlights and checked my speed . . . 81 kph . . . and . . . and

here it came -- the final curve . . . closing my eyes and locking my elbows, I revel in the momentary darkness . . .   I see Reema holding Anita, she's smiling, beckoning me forward.

<Kerrrrrash!>

Thrown backwards in my seat, the butterflies flew from my stomach to my ears, and my closed eyes saw me joining my family

                                                                          again,
                                                        at last.

In that moment, I knew I had done the right thing.
*   *   *
                                                                          Pulling

                          Rising
                                                                          Slowly
                    Fiercely

                    The thick, mercurial fluid formed into a pool at the mountain's peak.
            Bubbling, flowing from within the rocky giant itself, a rounded, silvery head
                                        began to rise.

In mere moments, I had become.
        I felt her last breath.
        I understood her final anguish.
        I experienced his ultimate grief.
                                                Yet I was all of these, and
more.

Turning my eyes upward to the celestial sphere which filled the sky, I heard it call to me
        . . .

R   o   s   h   a
                          and it became my first word,
                                                it was me.

                    My reflective darkform somehow encompassed
                    all that sought justice, strength, intelligence, and
                    vengeance. Power pulsed through my limbs
                    and I raised my arms to release it.

Flames exploded to the heavens from my hands held high. The novaflare announced my presence and the coming of the Ka into this confused and misguided world.

As I lowered my arms, a deep pulse resonated across my body. It came from my left, my destiny lay at its origin. I set one foot forward and descended the mountain. Sliding, stepping, striding, and stalking, justice followed where I led, yet my destination remained as mysterious as my birth.

The pain of this triple death--daughter, mother, father--reflected greater deaths of love, hope, and joy. In that moment, the Patels' agony found consciousness and form as Rosha, meaning mother-sister-daughter-warrior. The innocence of Anita's infancy recast as instinctive, chaotic darkness given silvery, feminine form. Carrying anger in her right hand and vengeance in her left, Rosha gazed east and strode to her destiny.

*   *   *

8th Lunar Cycle, 2051
Somewhere in the Amazon Rainforest

"A'ight, Jackson, put yer back n'to it!"

The Black man's broad, brown shoulders glistened with sweat . . . he leaned against a large tree and pushed forward. Swiftly moving his arms around the trunk, Jackson planted a booted left foot firmly on the ground and wrenched the tree upwards onto his right shoulder. Whether Jackson or the tree groaned more in the effort is impossible to tell.

Jackson's face contorted with concentration, his legs bent in shaking support, he spun on his right foot and slammed the 20 foot tree to the dirt.

Dust, leaves, and small branches rain down all over his shaved head and bare, muscular upper body. All three guards laugh long and loud.

"Hey, Jacko! If we're'n a good mood, maybe we'll scrub ya down wit da wire brushes before we t'chrow ya back n'da hole!"

The pale-skinned, balding man's belly jiggled as he laughed at his own joke. The other two guards--one tall and dark-haired; the other, olive-complected, blonde-haired and short--just sniggered.

Jackson's almond eyes smoldered with a killing rage, yet his gaze never turned toward the guards. The electronic monitors on his wrists and ankles prevented any thought of threatening his tormentors. He had made that mistake in his first, and only, escape attempt.

He had dropped one of them (huhm, didn't even remember what he looked like) with a spine-snapping blow to the back of the head, but, with a simple press of a button, another guard sent a 300 volt charge of electricity through his body for an excruciating five seconds. Jackson still managed to raise his fist and stumble towards that guard, when the other upped the charge tenfold. The last thing he remembers from that day was the smell of his own electrified flesh.

Now, despite the anger that consumed him at their insults, Lawrence Jackson kept his head bowed and simply found another boulder to clear.

Nineteen years. 19 years -- he had spent as a one-man clearing crew. But he still didn't question his actions or his decisions. He enjoyed blowing up planes . . . then watching the body parts being dragged from the wreckage for identification. The screams and gasps of horror and disbelief soothed him many a night in the lockdown. Yeah, that concrete box could drive him mad with its immobilizing, shaped fit and alienating, sense-absent environment. 19 years--no light, no sound, no smell, no taste.

God--how long has it been since he TASTED something. IV feeds, processed air, soundproofing . . . the only sensation he had, he memorized fifteen years ago -- the particular texture of the concrete under each index finger. Found only with extreme effort in his wrists.   But it was all worth it.

4 planes. 783 people. Physical and spiritual deaths for no reason other than his whim.

He fought back a smirk at the thought, knowing they'd abuse him more if they saw it. Jackson rolled a medium-sized rock -- not more than 500 pounds and six feet in diameter -- down the side of the hill into the area he had cleared last week. He'd store the rocks he could use down there and dam the tributary river in two weeks.

The guards still glowered over him. Their hatred had become the only taste he knew   . . . even it had gone stale years ago. Even in his submission, they knew he resisted them. Jackson's slow, powerful strides; his continuous, unrelenting effort; the keen balance and smoothness in his motions . . . they all betrayed the wild, psychotic blaze that fueled his soul -- his very control reminded them of his strength and their fear.

"Yeah, they call me the lunatic. But I wonder what the villagers would think of the guy who had me clearing land for them? Who let me come within five miles of their precious families everyday? What would they think of him?" Jackson's thoughts swirled inside him . . .

<BZZZZZZK!>

Jackson growls as his limbs freeze and explode into flame simultaneously. Unable to command his body, he drops where he stands and rolls to the foot of the hill that he had been climbing.

"Ha-ha!!" This time it was the short guard who juiced him. But Jackson still doesn't look at them. He simply collects himself and rises -- brushing the dirt and twigs from his body roughly.

"Hey, boy! Wait jus' a second! Y'know yall can' jus' go up dat hill alone! Mitch, Sparky -- I'm wit 'im this time." Even though, Jackson didn't look up, he knew it was Blondie.

Dragging his still-numb limbs with nothing but force of will, Jackson knew Blondie wouldn't come within ten feet of him. Even these guys were smarter than that. Looking up the hill, Jackson focused back on the task at hand--clearing all the larger rocks so he could start digging down the hill itself. No shovel ... in all this time. Still, a couple days work -- max.

The sun no longer reflected off Jackson's body as the dry dirt clung to his swarthy, titanic form. Standing well over six-foot, he didn't blame people for being afraid of him. In fact, he had sculpted his body to accentuate his imposing nature. But now, this achievement was wasted, no longer his own. The punishment, a life of sensory deprivation and enforced labor, certainly made use of Jackson in ways he never would have conceived--mostly by helping people.

Jackson began to stack the trees that he uprooted. He'd roll them down in awhile, he thought. But then he noticed . . .
                        Blondie was standing on a rocky ridge . . . gesturing childishly down at his buddies. A rookie mistake, he'd only been 'on' for a couple months, but by the time the other two warned him, it was too late.

Moving like a baseball instead of a 250-pound rock, a boulder smashes Blondie off the top of the ledge and breaks several larger rocks loose. Instantly, there's an avalanche and all three guards are being pummeled in it. Swept down three sets of cliffs, the cascading rocks thunder down and pile onto the stones Jackson had set aside for the dam. Omnivorous silence consumed any possibility of the guards' survival.

Jackson knelt down to watch the dust settle. As he did, he ripped the anklet monitors from their moorings in his bones. Howling in anguish and bleeding profusely, he tore the bracelets from his wrists and hobbled into the dense brush.

Freedom drove his body into rapid motion despite the horrendous pain that throbbed in his forearms and lower legs. "They not taking me back!" he screamed, "Never!!"

Running full speed, branches and other various fauna scratched and cut his torso and arms unmercifully. From the position of the sun, Jackson guessed which direction was north. Two months earlier, Blondie had slipped and mentioned that he was "going south" to check on the boats. They yelled at him for two hours about that slip-up, and the next day, the brush changed. The clearing location switched. But they always came by the river, and, after almost 20 years of holding him, Jackson was willing to bet they just started taking him to the other side. "They never thought I'd actually escape . . ." The brilliance of Jackson's broad smile was equally only by the malicious gleam in his eyes.

*   *   *

As I cleared the edge of the rainforest, I couldn't believe I'd made it this far. I probably only got another twenty minutes before the back-ups get here . . .
            I'm taking the boat -- maybe I can lose 'em upstream somewhere. Climbing in, I realize I buried the keys with the pigs back at the clearsite. Hope they haven't changed the ignition wiring too much . . .   else this chase is over 'fore it started.
Two sparks . . . and the engine's running!
            "Oh-YEAH!! I'm DANGEROUS!!"
    I'm screaming and laughing and still not believing . . .
                            .
                            .
                            .

"I'M FREE!!"

        The boat hums out into the deep water, and I turn and head west, upstream.

The sound of the engine roaring at full throttle . . .
The feel of the smooth wheel vibrating with power . . .
The scent of the jungle and wildlife intoxicating me . . .
The taste of the salty water splashing on my face . . .
The sight of no guards taunting and hounding me !!!
                    "I'M ALIVE!!!"

Each moment was a liberation. Every breath a revelation!
        Never again . . .   (My thoughts on the last 19 years)
                    Never
                            EVER
                                    Again.

<beep>   <beep>   <beep>
        A red light flashing on the panel . . .

No, no, no -- you can't break down on me!

<beep>   <beep>   <beep>
Cheap, government issue crap!
I was almost . . .

<BA -   DA -   BOOOM>

free.

*   *   *

I placed my hand on the ground and pulled my feet underneath me.

Flames licked my body as I flew through the air . . . and my skin crackled as if awakening with new energy.

I . . .
remembered
     Lawrence Jackson.

But
I knew
He was no longer me.

Somehow, I had
a sense
of . . .

peace.

That -- Jackson had never known.

All of his life was indulgence and capriciousness.
Yet, these were absent in me.

No . . .   Not . . . absent.
Contained . . .
Balanced . . .
Somewhere inside me.
Jackson's dark, evil lurked
waiting for its moment
to escape
its chance
to consume
me.

But   am   My   cast   the
who   I?   gold   light   sun-

body   much   nearly
                like   radiant.

I was a Lightbringer . . .
              the golden light made me?

                                                                    Yes.

      the sunlight and
                  the flames   recast
                                        reconciled
                  Jackson's unbalanced form.
Gave him love, peace, hope that he never knew . . .

                                                          Sun Gazing
                                                          upon me,
                                                          it and I
                                                          knew
                                                          Danzuro,
                                                          mine name
                                                          is.

The Lightbringer . . . the balance
                  of the soon-to-be-birthed Ka.
                  Her energies were nearly aligned,
                        half a world away,   I felt her sense me.
                  Before even this moment, she knew and called to me.

Glowing, both inwardly and outwardly, I lifted myself from the ground and rose
above the trees . . . but slowly,
                  enjoying the sizzling, light-energies which composed my body.

      Too soon, duty prevailed
                  responsibility reminded
                              and I turned to my right.
      To the west, before me, await both personal and global destinies,
                              cadaceusally entwined.

*Jackson, consumed with glee at his escape, failed to recognize the
significance of the flashing red lights on the boat's dashboard. The
explosion threw him high into the air--an angel of flame arcing into the
sun. He should have died. In one sense, he did. When the flaming form
crashed into the forest, it was no longer Lawrence Jackson. Danzuro
rose to his feet, his golden body sparkling in the light as it filtered through
the tropical canopy. Danzuro means harmonious reconciler, lightbringer.
The evil of Jackson's soul transformed into a radiant love which flowed
constantly from his being.*

*   *   *

The water lapped gently over my silver feet. It was cool, yet my presence made it more   so. The clouds created a pewter ceiling which pleased me. And this ... rightfully   attendant ... silence stood with Heimdallian vigilance, stretching in all directions.

Though he was not yet visible, his swift approach was unmistakable. Typically, he planned an overdramatic entrance.

On cue, a rainbow punctured the clouds and a dazzling, golden form descended from
        the heavens. Born mere moments ago, he lacks the disdain for pretense I have
        cultivated. I must teach this one effectiveness over showmanship, first and foremost.
The goal takes precedence over the effort.

.

.

.

Unflinching at my arrival, her complex simplicity struck me immediately. Her air of annoyance at my rainbow underscored my understanding of her focus.

Whereas I commanded notice everywhere I went, she desired only the subtle essence
        of silence. I must show her the joys of spontaneity and exuberance that are the birthright of our existence.

How and why are the ancestors of who, what, when, and where.
*   *   *

I was born on an unremarkable patch of ocean.
Rosha's silvery feet planted firmly on the lapping waves.
Danzuro's golden body floating placidly above the surface.
There were no words.

Only a touch.
Rosha reached up.
Danzuro reached down.
For the first time, I saw.

.

.

.

To the observer, both became hazier figures, blurred by a visual static.

As Rosha's form rose from the sea, Danzuro's descended towards it. Joined at the hand physically, they had become a spiritual one,

me   --   Ka.

And from where I stood, a pulse of platinum energy flashed outward, spreading its circular field to the ends of the planet.

The pulse magically swept the ill of humanity from existence. Greed, persecution, insensitivity, and hatred disappeared. Suffering, disillusionment, and disappointment all faded into history. Expression and choice, in the interest of a community of equals, became valued above all.

.

.

.

But the Utopian Era was shattered not one year after its birth.
    For as I glided over the same watery patch that birthed me, where Rosha and Danzuro joined -- I was frozen in place.

Slowly, my mind
            began to
                    split
                        in half.
                        Rosha and
                            Danzuro's formative
                                personalities
                                    began to reemerge,
                                        and I . . .

I
was lost.

*   *   *

All at once, I awoke . . . as if from a dream,   it had been mere moments from the initial union of the Ka, yet I also knew a year had passed.

"Why was I here?   Why can't I feel Dan -- "
        the response interrupted my question as a swirling, black whirlpool opened in the ocean beneath us.

        A Darkness-Well !!

        It roared and whooshed and drew me down into its vortex with a magnetic attraction.

Danzuro still seemed dazed as he did not even look at the spinning, ebony mass.

Tendrils lash upwards from the pit, grabbing my legs -- sending surges of pleasure through my chromeform -- My resistance plummeted, and my body began to follow.

"Danzuro!" My shout went unanswered as the pit, pulled both of us into its upper lip . . .
                    But -- if it gave me pleasure,
                                        it might kill Danzuro . . .

This couldn't be happening . . . I needed to let go, before the pit consumed
Danzuro's light . . .
                    already he had grown darker . . . his brilliant gold dimmed to a supple
bronze, as some darkness within him struggled to break loose.

            Then I noticed . . . the worst of all . . . as we were drawn further in,
the pit sent out pulses which reversed the utopia the Ka had created -- the chaos
of the previous age scored retribution for its censure, corrupting all it could in its
reborn freedom.

                                        And part of me rejoiced at this victory,
                                            but I knew it was wrong . . .
                                                out of balance . . .
                                                without Danzuro.
With   all   of   my   strength,   I   pulled   one
                                                    then
                                        two
                    of my fingers . . .
                                from Danzuro's hand.
            And he felt it!   He finally noticed!!!
                    But he's trying to reconnect . . .
NO!
NO!
NO!
NO!   I separated a third finger . . .
                                            only two more . . .

Confusion flashed across his brass features,
                            I hoped he would understand this .
. .

            I unleashed a blast of pure kinetic force from my hand through his --
    and the dark whirlpool amplified the strength of the blow, creating an
enormous
        explosion.

"NOOOOOOOOOOOOOOOOOOOOOOOOO!"

Danzuro's cry did not prevent him from tumbling out of sight,
                                    out of the Well's lethal reach ...
          head over heels, he flew   and   I   …
                         I fought my way, climbing back up
               the edge of the pit to pursue him.

But it was far too late.

                                              The tendrils still had me.
                          And the contact with the walls of the Well,
reinforced their grasp on me.

          My body racked with agonized euphoria,
               I surrendered to the pit,
               and watched the midnight sky
               become a pindot, then vanish,
          in the wake of my ecstatic Blackness.

*   *   *   *   *

ORDER

1st Lunar Cycle, 2052
Ten Kings District off the Potomac River

Breathing sand, pushing and pulling the grit past my lips. the subtle wind from my chest is all the motion that I can generate.

> what
>   happened   to
>   me?!?

I feel sooo cold... colder than any ice.... where am I? why can't I see? where is my body?

I
cannot
feel
anything!!!

Don't panic... think,   ... Rosha... The Ka... flying over the ocean
                  remember

we were frozen in place... suddenly, unexpectedly... and then
                           then
                    then

ROSHA WAS TORN FROM ME!
THE KA WAS SHATTERED!
        and   all   that   we   had   accomplished   began   to   fade.

The explosion of separation sent me into shock.... everything faded to white.... my memory fails me...

      the wind slashing by me like a blade,
                  I'd never flown so fast... WHAT HAPPENED???

      My body burnt its way through mountains in its flight trajectory...   until
until

my fiery form lost its flame... but, my explosive velocity barely diminished... my form shattered the
barriers it met,
          but at least I began to slow .....

Finally, after feeling airborne for months.... where is ROSHA?!? i crashed into deep

water...   finally   finally   finally
          consciousness mine heavy surrendered oblivion sank I
                                                            sank and

                                                        sank and
                                    sank

But now... I awaken
                    only able to breath and barely that....

"Ye! Dete!?" (Apollyonian translation: "Hey! You dead!?")

          A foot nudged my side...

"Ete munh?" ("Are ya human?")

          I manage a moan...

"Oemcn... tle tephep... leami ne tgra, n'slacien y uqe toehe."
("C'mon... lemme help ya up... my place ain't great, but s'warmer than out 'ere.")

          I'm rolled over, and I see a male... not too old, not too small, not too weak ....

                    he's ...   . smiling at me... ??

"Te olk vnecher, ra... He upeees rane ohtgrote... uospse donemwaps emcn otrocls y
mfphs esyds..."
("Ya look purty bad there, fella... I can see almos right thru ya... s'pose the world's
chil'un comin all culuhs and shapps these days...")

          his rags denote him as one without a home

"Nmec... he sopfor, plees, y rocm ewt phte vlo te ntas..."
"C'mon... I gots shelter, bed, and food to help ya back on yer feet..."

          The word echoes through my mind....   FOOD
                                                          FOOD
                                                          FOOD
                                                          FOOD

Before he can react, I've grabbed his outstretched hand. The hunger instantaneously consumes me, HE IS SO WARM!!! and i am sooo cold....

the strength of desperation powers my grip as I begin to drain the life-giving heat from his body...
at first slowly,   quasi-solid tendrils penetrate his skin and crawl through his veins

but he begins to struggle to escape...   reaching his core and letting me drink deeply his heat

  so I devour him swiftly   his scream cut short as I absorb even the sound
        providing no chance of escape...

in a matter of seconds, the color drains from his skin...
                    the moisture from his cells...
                    the heat from his heart...   my moment of succulent
satisfaction

the man's jaw drops swiftly, yet before it reaches its nadir, there is no flesh covering it....
his eyes explode like shriveled raisins
his skin falls like melting snow from his bones
                    as they chip
                        and crumble into dust on the sand beneath my
knees.

Momentarily sated, I rise to my feet... a struggle still... despite my feeding
my form is no longer transparent -- merely a jaundiced yellow... and my strength is
nothing like it   should be...
the feeding was necessary...
                    I would have died without it...
                            yet there was something
wrong...

"Aaaaarrrrrrgggggghhhhhh!!!!!!!"

Such thoughts are driven from me as the hunger plunges its spear through my abdomen again;

            I stumble up the beach--struggling against duplicating my first sound--
            towards the bright lights in the distance to find a new source of
                    sustenance.

*   *   *

Too long it has taken me to reach this place.
People pass me and glance not at all.

Viewing them, I see first packages of heat and energy... morsels for my
sustenance... but also   ...
          hollow, defeated, soulless vessels produced by their omnipresent desperation.

Since entering Ten Kings District, I have had hundreds of opportunities to consume
all that I could have --- but I have not.

                    These shells will provide little satisfaction for my hunger.
                    But the eerie feeling of wrongness chirps on my shoulder like the
          cricket   of   conscience.

Yet the hunger still gnaws away at my insides as if I were truly flesh and bone
instead of light
made
                                                                  solid.

After more hours of tortured wandering, I collapse in an alleyway... defeated and
subsumed by
my hunger... ready to turn to my last source of energy
                                        ...my own body...

But, I notice
          a small child hidden behind a pile of refuse.
          playing hide and seek...
                              despair has not destroyed all...

golden hair... reminds me of my true appearance...
                                        how I should be!!

                              .
                              .
                              .

                    The hunger throbs incessantly within me
          the child doesn't see me
                    I pounce on him
          he is soooo warm
                    I plunge my intangible hand into his chest
          Fear has frozen his voice
                    the draught of his life-energy both refreshing and intoxicating
          a scream implodes and dies as its wind is stolen
                    the heat restores more of my photon form
          his Azure eyes fade to ebon then deep iron gray
                              then almost transparent white

"Aaaaaahhhhhh...."

But I need more....

much more.

more

more

more

My maize form slides effortlessly down the alley and back into the street for the hunt.

*   *   *

A few blocks away, I sense

a fire rages, destroying a store.

Once there, I see   outside,   six young people

beat

"Lotarb!" ("Old Bastard!")

kick   "Te awt ro? Te awt ro? Se..

Se...Se"

(You want more? You want more?

Yes..Yes..Yes")

stomp

"Osn ket tod soed!"   spit on

("We own all that is yours!")

and thoroughly victimize an old man.

He stops moving

and they cheer... something deep inside me cries

out

and I do not know why....

Curious, I follow the gang... and its trail of pain, suffering, and sadness.

They terrorize the elderly, the sick, the infirm.... Soon

their trial of

vengeance, anger, and

retribution

shall come to pass.

For their bodies -- consumed with passionate rage, hatred, and violence will

make a much   much   better meal than the helpless and the weak I

have enjoyed thus far.

Among the six, there are four females and two males...

(they enjoy taunting their prey...)

None having seen more than a quiversnumber Solar cycles.

(as they abuse....)

All are disfigured and consumed with the violence of this world.

(and defile them.)
                    Often for nothing more than money or mindless pleasure
                    do they torment the hapless souls unto death.

An old man here,
        a young couple there,   a family in an apartment,
                        a man in his office

                                                no one is immune or safe.

Hapless Souls...   all of them...
            why? How did this come to pass?
        -- Somehow, I feel....
                        I KNOW

                    that it is MY fault.... the Ka...
                                        Rosha...
        Did our Disunion cause this??

                                    BUT THE HUNGER!!!
AGAIN!!!
I cry out in pain...
                        I WAS MEANT TO BE MORE THAN DESTROYER!!!

But my needy weakness is too great.
                    but the weight of responsibility haunts me like banshee...
            its wail chills me as much as the hunger.

The gang humiliates person after person
                        and I do nothing save end the misery
            of the crippled and the maimed...
                            while restoring the energy to my solid-
photon
                                        body.

        As in distant memory, I now float once again.
        Soon these spiritually barren adolescents will know the wages of their sins.
        My full being shall be restored.
        Too bad there is no way to fill their spirits with joy; perhaps then life and death
might have

been different.

But they are not. . .   and how strange that I might wish it so . . .

my power is not responsible . . . and such thoughts are ridiculous . . .

My chase and my hunger shall both soon end; that is all that matters.

*   *   *

Droogs . . . a foul name even for desolate souls such as those in the gang.
Its very

sound resonates with ignorance and apathy.
                                        I care nothing for any of them.

The ultimate price for their violence shall soon exact itself through me.

Silently I have followed. . .
Faithfully I have pursued. . .
                now I dim my glow and float to the roof of the Droogs' home
                        a warehouse mere yards from the beach where I laid
                        dying . . .

Melting a small hole in the metal roof, I spy their conglomeration.
        There are hundreds of them!
                all different colors, sizes, and ages. . .

The Disunion could never have caused the fragmentation that spawned such
hate and despair in those so young!!

                                        could it?

My body roars as the hunger ravages it once again -- casting any thoughts of
responsibility to
                                the wind.

I must be whole again.
I must find unity.
I must find peace.
I must find . . .   Rosha   . . . wherever she may be.
        and I cannot find her until I am complete.

These 'Droogs' must PAY for their collective crimes!

Below me. . . the gang members begin swaying left and right

--gyrating among the wealth they have amassed from others--

a mantra rises from their collective voice

--an offensive shriek celebrating their own lavascious excess--

"Doglr reosn! Qien indotma fleto!" ("Glory be to us! Who dominate Life itself!)

some light torches and burn incense around the building

. . . a man visibly drugged and nearly unconscious is brought to the center of
the

ceremony. . .   the members raise axes, knives, clubs, machetes . .
.

weapons of every sort . . . above their heads

I reach out and fan the sparks from the torches and incense.

. . . the gang encircles and approaches its victim...

The sparks begin to leap -- one by one -- into flame.

. . .Droogs chant louder and faster
                louder and faster
                louder and faster . . .
I feed the flames until Fire touches the crates within the warehouse
        surrounding the fanatically entranced Droogs.

. . .The first blows land on the man -- the only cries are for more blood from
the
                Droogs . . .

I can brook no more!!
                I burst through the ceiling -- exploding the fires into an
INFERNO!

Flaming crates tumble down upon Droogs from every side.
        For them, there is no escape.
The heat alone spontaneously combusts their ragged clothing.
        The living pyres shriek and dance and pirouette in a deadly ballet.

The chaos, heat, light, and flame all feed me. . . . and through all of them I drain away the life
                   energy of the Droogs.

        As I descend, the strong among them recognize my presence,
and, through their insanity, rush at me to end their misery.

            The first Droog... a girl the complexion of night...charges forth with a sword
        I blast the head from her shoulders, leaving only fused patch where her neck
used to be.

            The second Droog drove a javelin against my back
                            dismayed he was, as it melted on contact
        his death came as I raised his ambient body temperature
                                    to 300 degrees Fahrenheit
            reducing him to so much pudding

    In their final anticipation of death, all those that still live attempt to stampede me
                        from all sides...
    Sadly, the flames I call forth from all corners of the room move still swifter--
and fells every last one, no closer than 10 feet from my now shimmering and golden
                        form.

        As the smell of burnt flesh rises, I turn my attention to their intended
sacrifice--

Too late. . . he passed the way of all meat before I entered the fray . . . and, as his
body ignites
        from my touch,

                                        browning from chalk white
                                            to, finally,
                                        charred ebony,

a subtle irony strikes me.

I have done the Droogs a favor.
    They were not simply actors in a world of pain.
        They were also its victims.
        Their actions were reflections of their experiences.

            BUT THERE IS SOMETHING ELSE.

                            The thought bursts into my mind.

Firefighters have arrived to combat the blaze.

    I increase the heat to evaporate the water from their hoses before it can enter the

                                                building,

and stop my feast.

              BUT THERE IS SOMETHING ELSE.

                                   The feeling erupts through

me.

           in the base memories and emotions of the Droogs

                         the firefighters

                    even . . .

                            me. . .

there is a memory . . . a common memory . . . of happiness . . . of unity

    that is nowhere to be found in their conscious minds and current beings. . .

            I

                see Rosha

                       and me

     joined

          as I remember. . .

We were the focus of the happiness . . . It was our creation. . .

      which means

                the Disunion,

                and the darkness of this world,

                                        are

                                        my

                                        fault!!!

The darkness   NO!

in my core   NO!

laughs   NO!

I remember now. . . NO!

        I didn't have to   NO!

        destroy anyone   NO! NO!

                              I could have healed

                              them all!

Why
didn't
I
see
this
sooner?

So blind,   so selfish,   so weak. . .
        all of these and more was I.

   I call back all the flame and heat and light
                        into my body.   .   . too late for the Droogs
        but not for the firefighters and the rest of the city.

   The grief I feel, I channel into a blast that evaporates the metal roof.
        Racked with guilt, I shape the energy as a sculptor would stone.

        Let the planet behold the agony of a dream betrayed.
        The golden, agonized statue reflects my form too well against the nightsky.
for one brief moment, I illuminate the city, the nation, and the world

                            .

                            .

                            .

but the moment passes, and my flash-effect sculpture fades back into my small
form.

                A charred mass burialground --which used to be a warehouse--
surrounds me.

The flames are extinguished and the firefighters slowly advance towards me.
        My heart cries out to Rosha,
                and faintly,
                        her response carries to me from the far Northwest.

I gently lift myself from the ground.
                I recognized in one moment what my destiny was.
                        and, for that moment, I realized it.

        But re-illuminating the world is to be my legacy, no longer my destiny.
        And Rosha is essential to the task.

For I now understand,
                I will never, can never, be complete without her.
                                Nor she without me.

The Ka must be reunited,
                and I must atone for the sadness, death, destruction I have created
both here

                                                                                and

everywhere.
"Ay! Olv! Ustp!" ("Hey! Come back! Stop!)

The yells and appeals of the firefighters recede behind me slowly.
                They cannot follow me as I float higher and further away.

                but, in my mind, I promise to restore the happiness and peace
                                that is the world's birthright.

The hunger no longer afflicts my golden form.
But the ache of responsibility has marshalled
its strength from my knowledge of the truth.

                        Still the ache is much more welcome
                        than the surrender that the consuming
                        darkness at my core requires.

                                        Such evil will ever tempt me, but
                                        I am the Lightbringer. And my
                                        responsibility requires much more.

        *   *   *   *   *

CHAOS

They peel back painfully,   my eyes.

Instinctively,
          I spring backwards -- expecting   on my
                                    an attack   prone
                                                             position.

                                                   Looking forward
                                                   an empty corridor
                                                   glares back at me.

My soul
          reaches out to embrace
the darkness
                    before me.
                              .
                              .
                              .
                                        Yet it does not respond.

Forward
stride I.   .   .
                                        puzzled.

                         <KLA-BLAM!>

                              a metallic wall crashes down behind me

Cautiously .   .   .
               (A unique curiosity in my experience)

Confidently .   .   .
               I rush forward into Blackness mine.

                         <KLA-BLAM!>
                         <KLA-BLAM!>
                         <KLA-BLAM!>
                                                   wall after wall
               deny any reconsideration
of my charge forward

                    Repels me
                                        Rejects me
          Retreats from me

does yet the darkness do.
"I AM Darkness! Come forth to me!"
my cry Ignored.

I step forward . . .
measuring the response from my surroundings.

in -- spir -- a -- tion

Jumping as high as I can,
I expect to soar over one of the walls.   .   .   .   .
denied again overconfidence
is my   the walls extend everhigher
than even my apogee.

.

.

.

then   begins
my   Icarian
ascent

<KR-RUNCH!>

Why   did not   is a
the floor   my impact   cannot answer .   .   .
collapse at   question I
wonder

worry

Where is Danzuro?

What has happened to me?
Echoes of voluminous silence reply.

and again,
one foot falls in front

as the other follows.

<KLA-BLAM!>
<KLA-BLAM!>
<KLA-BLAM!>

*   *   *

Have I walked?

For hours?

For seconds?

For years?

For months?

Have I walked?

Ceaselessly forward,
I have marched.
No sign
of
anything else.

Save my prison and me.

I remember,

being pulled

--

from Danzuro . . .

masses of swirling darkness
embraced me

the joy which swept me

I knew

would kill
Danzuro. . .

But
he
was

just　　　　　　　　　　　　　　　　　　　　　　　　gone.

　　　　　　　　　　　　　　　　　　　　　　probably dead.

　　　　　　　　　　　　　　　　　　　　　　Deep inside

　　　　　　　　　　　something

howls
at that thought.

　　　　　　　　　　　　　　　　.

　　　　　　　　　　　　　　　　.

　　　　　　　　　　　　　　　　.

Am I dead?

　　　　No.　　　　　　　　　　　I am thinking.
　　　　　　Thought is life.
　　　　　　　　　　I'm thinking;　　　I
　　　　　　　　　　　　　therefore, LIVE!

Monotonous steps follow melancholy strides.

　　　　　　　　　　　　　　　　　　　No turns.
　　　　　　　　　　　　　　　　　No inclines.
　　　　　　　　　　　　　　No stairs.
　　　　　　　　　　No variation.
　　　　　No end.

This corridor taunts me with its fleeting darkness.
　　　　　　　　　　　　　　　　And I chase it.
　　　　Because it is all I have ever wanted.
　　　　　　　　　　　　　　All I ever have known.

　　　　　　　　　　　　　　　　So it goes . . .
　　　　one step cautious

　　　　　　　　　　　after

　　　　one step worried

　　　　　　　　　　　after

　　　　one step wary

after

                                                                another.

                Soon, the silence screams.
                and i raise my voice to join it.
        "YAAAAARRRRRRRRGGGGGGGGGGHHHHHHHHHHHH!!!"

*   *   *

Finally; beloved, undespised, silence
        regains its appeal

                        and, with it, returns my sanity

        but for how long?

I walk forward once more, trying to believe I
                        am   not
                        dead,
        when I see
IT!

                                        A ...   TURN!

Though walls slam behind me still . . .

                at last, SOMETHING NEW!!

        after a few steps into the turn, the walls
                resume the obstruction of my previous path.

                                But a breeze gently caresses my silvery
body.
                The nigh inaudible hiss of the wind,
                        nearly brings tears to my eyes.

Wait.

That's ridiculous!

I've never been so emotional.
What is

happening
to me!?!

.
.
.

Meaningless Time
has become my
white-gray tomb.

Life has become a burdensome ennui. Every
moment, a strange emotion threatens
to shatter my tenuous hold on lucidity.
Not even the simple, occasional turns bring me joy any longer.

Joy. What an
asinine concept.

Yet it felt so
good.

Enough!
Such thoughts
do nothing
for me . . .
Step
<KLA-BLAM>
Step
<KLA-BLAM>
Step
<KLA-BLAM>

Strange . . .
the walls . . .
are becoming lighter,
whiter.

In
the
distance,
a
faint

SCREAM!

Not even my own!

I dash forward!
Emotions flow through

me like nothing else!!!

I DON'T CARE!!!

Running forward, the darkness retreats til it is merely
a pin dot in my imagination.

I block the sound of crashing barriers from my ears.

Faster   to platinum
    and   walls fade
       faster   the

thought   platinum
    than   fades
      swiftly   to
        more   white
          until I
          am running
          on nothing

          moving
          neither
       forward nor backward
        up nor down
        left nor right.
   I keep running.
                     <The screams get a little
louder>
   I won't stop!
                     <A little louder>

the white space begins to strobe
                     <Louder still>

I'm almost there!
                     <From just ahead>

   i stumble
      blinded by the strobing corridor.

I yell, "Don't Stop!"
Crashing sideways against a white surface, I
scramble forward.

The room spins!

<shrieking from above me>

I fall to my right,
but
no sooner than I land,
I am thrown over to my left . . .

I can hear words . . .

<NO! STOP!>

I jump at a wall . . .

<PLEASE!>

I guessed well . . .
. . . I don't slam into anything . . .

<GET AWAY!>

but didn't act fast   -thump-

Rotating, strobing corridor --
will not stop me
from finding that voice . . .

<NOOOOO!>

-Thump-
-Crash-
-Bang-

it's too fast!
I can't get my bearings!

Screams mingle with slaps and thuds
bombarding me from all sides

along with a deep
laughter.

Rage consumes me.
But I still can't see what's happening . . .

Falling again, I am.
Expecting to slam into
the ceiling,
I was.

But instead, I feel nothing as
the screaming abruptly stops and
the blinding white fades to gray.

*   *   *

"Uhhh . . . "
I moan as I plant my hands on the floor and lift myself.

My only hope, that I was not back where I started.

groans and grunts
break my train of
thought.

Their sound is familiar.

Turning my head,
I locate the noise's
source.

A large male stands above a crumbled body,   gesturing
threatening.

his pale hand
<Crack!>
slaps down on the body's head.

The slight moan   the body is   I sought.
confirms that   the screamer

Again
        &
Again
        &
Again
       the male savagely lashes on the woman's motionless form.

                                                    My insides
                                       pulse with
                         her heartbeat.
      Hisfistcrossesherfaceatspeed.
                         <Krrrrrnnnnchhh>
      Butitismyjawthatbreaks.

(and I fall to my knees in shock)

<Thud>
      Hisfootembedsinherchest.
                      <krik krak krak>
      Yetitismyribsthatcrack.

                      (rolling on the floor I have never felt such
pain)
Over and over,
      he shatters limb after limb.

  My screams echo hollowly all around me as our broken bodies grind and tear.
  With my last strength, I draw a pewter javelin from my body and cast it at the
attacker.

The sound of the shattering spear is overwhelmed only by the siren-shrieks of the
now-   conscious woman.

"You wanna scream, slut!?," howls the Horror, "I'll give you something to scream
about"

                      .
                      .
                      .

      Snatching her by her neck, both her and my bodies are lifted from the
ground.

He licks her face.   The moisture runs down my cheek.
He tears her pants.   The sting rips my hips.

He squeezes her throat.   The air flees from my lungs.
He breaks her hyman.   Yet I feel his dick.

Faster   He
     and   violates
Harder   us ...

          Over and over,   we scream.
          After a while,   we stop
                    and surrender to the silence of his dream.

My
          Tears
          trickle,
                    then stream,
          down my face.

                                                              His
                                                            Sweat
                                                           swirls,
                                                      then streaks,
                                                   twin serpents
                                                              down
                                                          my arms
                                                          my torso
                                                          my legs
                                                          my feet
                                                          my toes.

                              He's
                          inside me   before his
                              for   fluid
                            Years   flows.

          but the stink of
          his breath remains.

His grip doesn't slacken.
                    It tightens.   "NOOOOOOOOOO!"
I howl as I struggle forward,
                    slamming my broken fists against the invisible wall that
                    made me witness this holocaust while

denying my ability to stop it.

Against this barrier, my spirit splinters into more pieces than my spear had.

<snap>

broken her neck He has.   I tumble to floor, expectant.
           The numbness of death overcomes me.

     And now, we both shall die.

   Entirely broken, we cannot even scream.
   Fitting somehow, that the silence of life
     ushered us both unto death.

.
.
.

But it does not come for me.   Though the woman's pulse has left
me.

I still cannot move!

      She is gone.

Throwing her corpse to the floor, he says,
   "Well, you were finally good for something."

his	robustly	my	cold,	his	my
laughter	and	soul	just	violation	body.
echoes	freezes	ice	as	froze	

Arrogantly picking his nose, he strides away.

  the further he gets,
  the more I can move.
I try to stand.
    But even with him gone, it is difficult.

         I feel so weak,
          so drained.

every movement is a test of will.

<KLA-BANG!>
the walls slam together around me.
Once again, leaving me only one

path.

Forward.

.

.

.

After hours of effort,   I can walk   .   .   .

haltingly   . . .
but I'm walking.

"Whoa!"   <Crash!>
I stepped forward too quickly.
and my rigid body fell to the floor.

Struggling to rise again, I swear . . .

That man's suffering,
for the rape and death
of my woman-sister,
shall be the stuff of legend.

.

.

.

My thoughts of vengeance are interrupted by a faint humming.

maybe
singing?

In my rush to rise quickly and hear it,
I crash back to the floor.

Then,
I notice . . .
the sound comes from
beneath me?

Turning my head, I see a metal grate emerging from the floor, lifting me an inch off the ground.

the song,
        more like a chant,
is much louder.

It is familiar.

Very familiar.

Slowly,
        Bodies bone white,
                yet well-muscled, complete their ascent
                        from beneath the metal floor   ...

Moving through the steel as if it were air, I see three move to either side of
                                                my prone body.
                                Their faces are featureless,
                                Yet their rhythmic repetitious
                                        chant does not cease.

Where have I heard this before?

        Something is poured over me.

                        Perhaps this is a primitive blessing?

The rage at my helplessness here does not reach a boil.
                        There is something
                                soothing
                                hypnotic
                                about

AAAAH!

I thrash about wildly on the grating as flames dance along my form.

        I cannot rise,

                                I cannot run.

I can only wail as the bodies lift the grate, with my flailing body upon it.
Placing this pyre on their shoulders, these figures carry me away.

My
skin
bubbles
and
pops.

        The smelting iron air fills my nostrils and my lungs.
        Metallic drops -- the remains of my body -- drip to
        the floor, rippling momentarily before being absorbed.

      My skeletal pallbearers ignore my thrashing
                         and   form.
          screaming

As my eyes melt,
and I cease moving,
two things remain with me.

The sight of the maze
absorbing my essence,
erasing any trace that
I ever was.

And the rhythmic chant   .   .   .
        "Ra-am   Na-am   Satya   Hai"
        (Hindi translation: God, thy name is Truth.)
        "Ra-am   Na-am   Satya   Hai"

        "Ra-am   Na-am   Satya   Hai"

      Soon, even that is gone and I have nothing.
        Not even the Blackness,
          so long loved,
          so long pursued;
          yet, in this maze,

never caught,
never experienced.

*   *   *   *   *

REBIRTH

3rd Lunar Cycle, 2053
Saskatchewan, Canadian Shield Region

Floating silently across the snow, he broods. The memories of what could have been, in the face of what is, are unbearable.

The snow melts to slush in the wake of his luminescent presence. If only he could transform himself so easily. The wind blows viciously across the flat, Canadian plain, but cold is a feeling denied the warmth of his being. If only his body shielded him from the biting gale of remembrance. Then, perhaps, he could know happiness and contentment again.

Land as bleak and desolate as his tormented soul extends in all directions around, yet he moves with a determination and conviction of one within sight of his goal. He knows he is responsible for all that has gone wrong in the world, and this journey is but another attempt to correct that failure. Awaiting him is a demon, a monster of darkness, not unlike the self that he left in Ten Kings.

Danzuro feels its presence as if it were a heavy fog hanging around him. As he nears the creature, reality blurs; chaos becomes as common as order, illusion becomes indistinguishable from reality. But Danzuro cannot stop. Perhaps there is another clue about the Restoration to be found here, and for that chance, he is willing to risk everything.

A town rises on the horizon ...

*   *   *

I approach the village with a vague feeling of trepidation. It even seems to grow with my every step, but I cannot turn back.

A thin mist is falling as I pass the first building--the first of many fur tanning stores. It is boarded up, and a brisk wind passes over me.

I continue down the main street of this town looking for any sign of life, but there are none to be found. No movement, complete stagnation. The mist thickens . . .

Wait.

Something.
I feel it . . . in front of me . . .

Out of the mist, a figure limps towards me. The timidity in my essence swells--
what's wrong with me? Why can't I see this thing? I cast my brilliant glow forward . . .

A woman stands revealed. Club legged and considerably aged, but a woman.

"Help me! My husband was attacked by the beast! You are the Lightbringer.
You can heal him!"

The first words of my native tongue that I have heard in this mad world,
and they state a need for my aid. Her words ring true inside of me, and my
determination, my obligation, to preserve life overwhelms my misgivings. I follow
the woman into a shallow alley where a body trembles, face down, in the snow.

The snow melts silently under my feet as I touch the ground. Kneeling over
the body, I reach out to spark any remnants of life within the victim.

I turn him over ... stunned at the null sensation that responds to my touch. I
feel nothing within him.

His face,   stripped
                           of all its skin!

Metallic his bare skull was!

                                        .

                                        .

                                        .

His foot strikes my stomach and sends me flying backwards across the
street, smashing through the front wall of the local tavern.

Slowly, regaining my bearings, I look up just in time to see this cyborg fire
twin, slim onyx darts at me from mountings in its arms. The spikes puncture my
hands--pinning me to the bar. The dark shafts hold me utterly immobile.

Then, I see them.
The bodies--everywhere. How did I not see them?

Littering the streets, impaled on hitching posts, hung from ceiling beams,
everywhere.

Some are quartered, others gibbeted, still others merely decapitated. The
poor

bartender's head dangles precariously over the bar next to me, only attached to his body by his spinal column, which stands revealed to the world.

Laughter--their laughter. I hear their laughter, and, for the first time, notice how dull my perceptions are and how nauseated I feel.

The woman and the cyborg walk into the bar, charged with delight at my revelation . . . at their successful deceit.

"Wakata-gu brolo! Aproptoshu." (Apollyonian translation: The Lightbringer is brought low, and by the products of his own failure. How appropriate.")

Laughter, derision, shame, determination.
I will not surrender so easily. Not to demons I have sworn to defeat. Not today.

Wrenching the obsidian daggers free of the bar, I leap onto the man-machine. The look of surprise on its face almost makes the effort worthwhile.

The momentum of my burst carries us into the snow-hidden, body-covered street. I pin its shoulders with my knees and drive the twin stilettoes, still pierced through my hands, through its gray eyes and into its electro-organic brain.

It jerks once.
I pull my hands off the back of the spikes.
It trembles once.
My stomach settles down.
It dies.
Strikes me from behind, she does.
The blow knocks me over on to my back where I can see her leaping at me.

I tuck my knees and "monkey-flip" her onto her back. Rolling over her, and pinning her as I had her partner, I hold her life in my hands.

"Lute hater. Eh Wakata-gu. Aktelow!" ("My soul is shattered! You're the Lightbringer -- make me whole!")

Her deceptive request echoes in my mind as I throw my fist through her open mouth and separate her head from the rest of her.

Silence.
The wind.
The ever-dense mist.

A voice.

"Azhooz, eh pucedetyarkn." ("Amazing how often, and well, you produce death and darkness.")   Laughter.

I rise, realizing that the true demon had just used me, deceived me with these two pawns. I could have, should have, healed them.

I leave the town, and a fog gathers in the distance.

*   *   *

Drifting further north, I feel the reverberations of the monstrosity's evil. The injuries from my village encounter vanished within moments of being inflicted, yet the haunting analysis of my actions weighs heavily on my mind.

Those two people needed my help; the woman even asked me for it. But all I could do was destroy them, blinded by my belief that they were corrupted by the darkness I created ... Darkspawn.

Maybe they were, maybe the Beast she spoke of claimed them as volunteers, but that does not excuse my unthinking actions.

I am the Lightbringer, Danzuro Ka; I will not make that mistake again.
                                             .
                                             .
                                             .
The fog has so obscured my vision that I can no longer see more than ten feet in any direction.

I am chasing the phantom feeling I get from the darkresonance of the demon, and that sensation grows exponentially with every stride.

I am totally vulnerable to the demon's attack. I hope this accursed fog affects its movements as well, but I suspect not. Nature itself seems to have turned against me as further punishment for my failures.

In this world of darkness, the environment is chaos' ally, and my foe.
I hear something.
The back of my neck crackles with anticipation. It is near.
The fog is thinning.
"Danzuro ..."
In front of me ...   .and down.
I float closer . . .
                    til . . . . THERE IS NO GROUND!

I manage to fall back to the snowy surface mere seconds before plummeting into the pit. The fog continues to dissipate.

The pit is black, jet black,
                        and has no discernable bottom.
"Danzuro . . ."
Again, from the pit. The demon is still unimaginably close--is it invisible? Why can't I see it?
The walls of the pit seem to move in a circular, swirling motion. Misty streaks of white and gray appear intermittently, randomly.
" Help me ..."

I know that voice, but I haven't felt her since . . .
"Please . . ."
               since I left Ten Kings.
The demon's tricks and games; it's here somewhere.
I look into the depths of the pit,   and see her.
    At the bottom, barely visible; I feel her.
Rosha.
    The key to the Restoration.
(The swirl of the pit almost pulls me in.)
      "Help me ..."
    The lost half of the Ka.
Somehow, the demon has imprisoned her. (Where is it?)
      "Please . . ."
The world needs us both. (I cannot go on alone.)
      "Reach out . . ."
I must help her.
      "Touch me ..."
I jump ...

The pit is chaotic confusion. I move in all directions at once. Its chaos is almost appealing to me. The gossamer whites and grays are the essences of the dead villagers--the demon must trap them here as well. Where is Rosha?

There, at the bottom, beckoning me closer, eager to be freed, desperate (like me) to reunite the Ka.

My fall accelerates with each passing moment, the swirling randomness of the pit spins faster around me, closing tighter and tighter as I approach the bottom.

Rosha's silver, smiling face grows larger on the horizon.

It reassures me.   For a moment.

Then the smile becomes sinister.

Rosha's face contorts and reforms as the Demon's face.

An amalgamation of both magical and technological evil.

"Wendigote, y fineh." ("I am Wendigo, and you are done.")

The silvery image, which I had pursued so doggedly, swiftly recedes into the distance until it is only a pin dot.

I continue to accelerate, but never getting any closer to my sterling speck.

Struck suddenly from all sides I am.

The chaos is reaching out. it and the slain village people.

They reach out, touch me--trying to make my light part of their darkness.

They envelope me, drain me, penetrate me, until all that I am is it and all that it is is me.

But it is not satisfied; within the pit, there can be no "me." And it attacks me in earnest; defenseless, I stop moving.

It taps my dark core, ripping it free of my bright carcass.

I am naught.

*   *   *

Cold.
Dark.
Paralyzed.
No.
Move.
Why.
Kill.
Why.
Because.
No reason.
Maim.

Better.	Slower.
Torture.	Happiness.
No.	Sadistic.
Wrong.	Who says.
Fight.	Hit.
Fight.	Move.
Run.	Help.
Drowning.	Frozen.

Surviving.   Stronger.
Weak.   When.
Now.   Help.
Who.   Me.
No.   Who.
Someone.   Honest.
Capable.   Warm.
Rosha.   Dead.
Gone.   No one.   Perfect.
Like her.   Me.   Alone.
Again.   Always.   Drowning.
Death.   Yield.   No.
Cowardice.   Bravery.   Balance.
Strike.   Power.Insatiable.
Hunger.   Relief.   None.
Peace.   Not.   Brain boiling.
Anger. Hatred. Prejudice. Wicked. Demon. Strength. Quickness. Power. Laughter.
Limitless. Infinity. Human. Love. Where. None. Gone. False. Find it. Now. Work
harder. Die. Strive longer. Escape. Fly higher. Hope. Battle. Challenge. Fight.
Unbound. Penalties. Anger. Binding. Escape. Rim. Move. Hide. Confront.
Strike. Hit. Kill. Maim. Destroy. Crush. Die. Die. Die. Hurt. Pain. Inflict. Escape.
Please. Help. Not fair. Endless. Work. Everpresent. Omnipresent. Smile. False.
Frown. Spit. Greet. Hit. Why. Frightened. Unaware. Alone. No one. Help. Me.
Help. Everyone. Silly. Smiles. Happiness. Bullshit. Trust. Respect. Love. Stress.
Wendigo. Work. Death. Peace. Satisfaction. Life. Good. Get it. Get up. Endure.
*   *   *

"Arrrrgggggghhhhh!" (Is this what it feels like to be born?)
Breathe. (I'm out of the pit!)
Deep breath. (It must have rejected the darkness in my soul!)
Open my eyes.
Snow, beautiful snow!
Where am I?
What do I feel?
Warm, tender,   wrong. . .
WENDIGO.

I rise to my feet and look around. It is everywhere. The demon's presence
is an ambient cloud, electrifying me, driving me crazy. The fog slowly creeps in
again.

I am standing at the edge of the pit. Again, it swirls around and around in its
hypnotic, chaotic symmetry. Again, it calls me.

"Danzuro": And it winks its silvery eye.

But I will not yield. I escaped its consuming substance once, and subsequently experienced birth trauma. I have no desire to attempt to be so lucky again.

Wendigo.
    It's here, but where? I feel it in the pit, I saw it in the pit, but it wasn't there . . .

Up.

    Looking up, I see the answer. A pillar of platinum-colored metal hovering about 500 feet above the center of the pit. Focusing on it, I confirm the feeling of destiny which awaits me on the pillar.

The fog rises quicker and thicker.

    Setting my feet on the ground, I take a fifty meter running start and jump again from the edge of the pit. But this time, upwards and outwards. (Knowing that I could only float so high and hoping that the momentum from my jump would carry me to the bottom edge of the pillar.)

                                    .
                                    .
                                    .

<KaChunk>
<Hssssss>

    My hands generate enough heat to burn into the metal like it was ice. I carve handholds in the pillar to make my way upward.

    Looking down, I see nothing but fog. The pit still calls me, pulls me. I look up and begin to climb.

<KaChunk>
<Hssssss>
<KaChunk>
<Hssssss>
<KaChunk>
<Hssssss>
*   *   *
    Hours of painful climbing, through the fog, against a biting wind, my illuminating glow fades to almost nothing. Only will propels each hand after the other. Hailstones beat me over the last 250 meters, but my hand still finds the upper ledge.

I pull myself onto the top, drained from the exertion. Slowly, so slowly, the warmth in my core seeps back out to my limbs. Life pulses through my every cell again as my icy coat of armor melts away.

Then I feel it.
Not merely everywhere, but also nowhere. The beast is out there, and in here, and everywhere in between.

"Eh itow, doeh?" ("You know it, don't you?")

Its breath is my breath is the wind is the mist is the pillar. We are one.

"Noeh casete." ("Now you may see me.")

I open my eyes wider. It is over eight feet tall--a monstrous shadow standing beyond a veil of mist.

I rise to greet it.

"Wakata-gu, daeh stayce moarkn?" ("Lightbringer, dare you stand and create more darkness?")

Rosha.
The village.
The world.
My fault -- all of it.
"Xah, Wakata-gu. Hoiapropty naareh ..." ("Yes, Lightbringer. How inappropriately you are named ...")

It laughs, an awful crackling sound. Its maw filled with shark-like rows of razor-sharp teeth. Hydraulic valves whine as it advances; cybertronic technology flashes beneath its matted white-gray fur; an air of decay hangs in its presence. It steps forward, towering over me.

"Ied, doehque esi stod alttehalu?" (Indeed, what have you done besides destroy all that you hold dear?")

Anger, depression, frustration.

"Eh brmiy akeh y treaspa en reseeh!" ("You bring misery in your wake and spawn hatred in your presence!")

It is right.

"Tehr mas, Wakata-gu ... o houl katte, 'Maula'?" ("We are the same, Lightbringer ... or should I say, 'Father'?")

My fist buries itself, burning, into its abdomen, disrupting its existence, removing that smug grin, sending Wendigo sprawling across the top of the platinum column.

The fog and hail are gone. Only the mist and rain remain.

"Seeh? Tureh se vilet, Maula. Aclo y reog senseh!" ("You see? Your very nature is violent, Father. Accept it and recognize your true identity!")

It leaps at me, electroferrous claws slashing my face and torso, leaving frigid gashes on me.

The battles then begins in truth. Each of us delivering terrible blows and causing horrible wounds. I do not tire; though I can barely see the Beast, my determination to destroy it is unwavering.

Yet it endures my onslaught with equal resilience and returns the punishment with comparable zeal. We *are* one.

I know what I am doing wrong.

"Seque ttem, Maula? Lowod deleh?" ("What's the matter, Father? Slowing down in your old age?")
Its body is hunched. Streams of petrolubricant and blood mix as they emerge from its mouth, its neck, and its stomach.

My body is tiger-striped with the Wendigo's onyx claw-slashes. My body seems sluggish and heavy.

This is the end for one of us. Our eyes meet, and I do not blink.

"Oijavtltehr." ("Let our battle be joined.")

Its voice cracks--it knows it is defeated. It leaps at me; I sidestep left, grabbing its right arm. I place it in a full-Nelson hold and force it to kneel; I kneel with it, barely maintaining my grip. It thrashes and struggles violently to break away, but I shall not let go.

I will not make the same mistake again. I envelop it with my warmth, my spirit, my essence. I open myself to its evil, capriciousness, and degradation. I flood it with the purity of love, honor, and truth. I accept its offerings of hate, deceit, and dishonor.

It trembles in its core at the exposure to the light.
I weep in my soul at my recognition of the dark.

"Roeon! Roeon!" ("No more! No more!")

Its cries go unanswered. The luminescence of my being takes its root in the core of the technodemon, just as darkness exists in the fundamental essence of my soul. The heat I generate vaporizes the necrotechnology that powers Wendigo. Its being is reborn.

The world around us is no longer significant. Once so intimately bound and defined by our struggle, our union has rendered reality meaningless; it seeks definition from this final action. We, Danzuro and Wendigo, define what is real for us. Rosha's face appears to me as the Beast takes its new shape. She kisses it and caresses me.

She smiles ...
and fades. I will find her.

"Waaaaaaaaaaaahhhhhhh!"
It is not my voice which cries out, nor is it Wendigo's. It is a new voice, full of innocence and purity.   On my knees, I open my eyes and look down.

.

.

.

The baby closes its mouth and opens its eyes to meet my gaze. Its eyes are golden, like mine, but its skin is platinum like Rosha's. I will call it Zodar because it carries my essence and Rosha's being.

It reaches up, touches my face, and giggles. A soft, gurgling sound not unlike that of a small stream. From such terrible evil, this pure innocence blossoms. I could not have done this without Rosha; her presence, reclaiming the chaos for just that instant, ensured this victory.

As for the pillar, the pit, and the village, after Zodar's birth, they all vanished. Either they never existed or existed only as extensions of Wendigo's power. It does not matter. Zodar and I now stand at the peak of a mighty mountain--green and verdant, full of life--a symbol of life's triumph over death here.

I pledge, "Here, on this mountain, the seeds of the Restoration are planted. Returning with your mother, we three shall cast the world back onto the path of peace and progress. This place is a harbinger of paradise, that is, for now, yours and yours alone. Be well and grow strong--the time for rebirth is nigh."

I set the child down in the shade of a willow tree, kiss it on the head, and smile at it.

It smiles back, so like Rosha's smile, and says, "As salaam alaykum." (Arabic translation: "Peace be unto you.")

*   *   *   *   *

Found

<plip>
        <plop>
<plip>
        <plop>

                                        . . . satya hai . . .
                            (Hindi Translation: ". . . is truth . . .")
                <plip>
                    <plop>

    . . . raam naam . . .
("God, thy name . . .")   <plop>
                                                        <plip>
                                                            <plop>
                                    . . . satya hai . . .

Liquid chrome drips from the smooth, metallic ceiling. Though the silver bullets' falls should echo, the collision with the floor resounds not.

Each bright gray bulb lands, then beads along the floor's surface.

        Then, almost
                    imperceptibly, the beads begin to bubble,
                                                then rise.
        Off the ground, slowly
                                    one
                                    at
                                    a
                                    time,
                                almost surreally . . .

then, their flights curving,
                the shiny orbs began to

                                            collide
                                            coalesce
                                                and
                                darken . . .

        somewhere, after several hundred
                    drops had silently merged,
                I awoke --
                        once again with a start.

I . . . felt   Danzuro touch me.   But he wasn't here.
            instead, a silver baby reached towards me   Is it really there?

and asked,

"Please . . . help me . . .   help him . . .
                    to help you."
                                    Confused, but
                                                    directed--I kissed the
child
whose eyes then glowed Danzuro's gold . . . it had never seemed more brilliant
                    and, an odd . . . warmth . . . flowed through me . . .

Where am I?

                    I blinked, and I was back in the maze.
                                    where helplessness crippled me for the
                                                    first time.
                    I almost wish I had melted into absence.

My hunger for justice,

                                    my pursuit of vengeance,

                    my unceasing march to perfection --
at last, they were all gone.
                                    No longer was I frustrated at that
                                    simultaneous impotence and violation.

                    Yet as the dropping orbs cast upwards and into my body, reforming it,
                    so too returned my responsibilities. . .
and, more importantly,
                                    my memories.
                                        .
                                        .
                                        .

            of the burning

                                                    of the spinning

            of the labyrinth

                                    and the rape.

Turning my head, I again face an impenetrable darkness . . .
            but I feel it more this time.   Somehow,
                                                    this darkness is mine.
            Out there, somewhere . . .
                        he roams,   gloating,

flaunting his dominance over me.

My second chance,

I will have to make him pay.

Strangely,
the Darkness recedes from me
quickly . . .
encouraging my pursuit.

I take a moment to feel my reunited form
to bask in the chaotic stability renewed . . .

to focus my attention on the violator.

The walls   I anticipate
rip past   each turn
in a blur . . .

I expect
each

incline.

the maze and I exist

now

in symbiosis

like never before.

what has changed??

Me?

My surroundings?

or

panting
gasping
in the distance,
My prey . . .

He's stumbling
            struggling
        running

through the darkness.

His pulse pounds as it races through his veins.
            I laugh   . . .   an explosive sound
            which sharpens his sudden inhalation.

The terror he feels . . .

knowing his end approaches . . .
is but a slight reflection of his wife's.

.
.

His sweating and breathing were in pleasure before,
                                        still,   the lesson I offer him has only
                        begun.

I slide silently across the metal floor . . .
                        he is just ahead   --
                                        collapsed,
                                                        nearly unconscious   --
                surrendered to the inevitable.

                Slowly,
                        I allow the wind's whistle
                                to amplify as it
                                        passes my outstretched arms.

I allow
                                                        my silver feet
                        to shriek at a pernicious pitch against the smooth surface
                                as they carry me to him   --
                announcing the passage and execution
                                        of my demonic justice.

                The sound seems to awaken the hunted
                                hunter

                and, with desperate strength, he again
                climbs to his feet and scrambles forward
                                into the darkness.

But I see him now . . .

                        ragged clothing,
                                        hanging from his
                                                gaunt, pale
                                                form . . .

So much weaker
than he was mere
momentous millennia
ago.

                        Danzuro would

want to
redeem this utter

trash   --

construct
something good
from
this base greed
and
abuse.

But he is not here.

I am.

And I know . . .
this beast is beyond
redemption.

Barefeet slapping against the
floor . . .

Hands alternately pushing and
pulling the feeble form
forward . . .

Caked solid, sweat
and
human excrement
are
this man's armor . . .

yet
all   it   he
repels   is   never
the   decency   earned.

Flashing images dance before my eyes as his
pleading screams
blend with
my
skating shrieks,
composing a symphony of justice.

And, inside me, the remnants of the battered woman

smiles

and

sings,

creating a harmony, that Danzuro would never comprehend.

Some crimes cannot be forgiven,
only punished.

Lost in the moment,
the man crawled further away
than I had intended . . .

Not matter . . .
with a thought,
the corridor pitches a 75-degree incline and
the protesting squeaks and squeals of the man's arms, hands, and feet
sliding down the cold metal
fill the air.

I stand at the ramp's base, smiling at his descent.
He rolls onto his back,
facing me as he hits bottom.

An act of final defiance . . .
his foot strikes my groin
with a
<CLANG>

(Given the opportunity,
"Shhhhhhiiiiiiiiiiiiittttttttttt!"
the shattered bone might have healed in a few LCs.)

My gaze upon him never wavers.

"I own you. Your resistance failed . . . from the first moment. Behold the pain you
inflicted . . ."

Extending a platinum blade from the top of my right wrist (its tip curving four inches from
my balled fist), I plunge my hand into his face.

Instantly,
I plant the
experience
of his violation
in his every cell,

Eternally.

> I rip the knife,
> back from his
> forehead
> and
> the wound
> closes
> behind it.

But this   . . .   man   . . .

> who destroyed

> without provocation
> or
> instigation

> who consumed with
> calculation
> and
> spite.

This man felt every atom of his being torn
> asunder

> - again   and   again-
> in a cascading torrent of agony.

> He writhed and screamed and shuttered and shivered
> at my feet . . .

> Limbs thrashing wildly, he begged for release and the eternal sleep.
But I will not allow it.   Every instant of the double violation he performed, THAT was
his experience -- in both infinite and infinitesimal detail.

Tears rolled down his cheeks and saliva sprayed from his mouth.
> When I felt he understood some small portion of his crime,
> I lifted him from the floor and held him.

His trembling, spiritually-drained body found
> only cold comfort
> in my everlasting arms.
Yet, I felt his gratitude for even that.

In that moment, I raised his face to mine
                              and kissed him deeply.

    His eyes opened wide with shock as
          he felt the Blackness of my being
          flow freely from my mouth into his
          throat.

    At first, he struggled . . . then the intoxicating
          pleasure of substance mine consumed
                    his will . . .

                    deep inside him, I planted a hunger,
                    an echo, and a vision.

My open eyes reached through the windows of his soul,
                    and marked him to forever
                              recall his transgression.

His stomach would never be sated, until he found his wife and apologized to her,
          begging her forgiveness. Forever he will wander this maze, seeking
absolution
          and satisfaction, chasing a faint residue of his wife's voice. When he finally
          does glimpse her, she will disappear around a corner, leaving only a molded
          scrap of bread. This scrap will increase the hunger tenfold each time he eats it,
          and the voice will call slightly louder--tantalizing his pursuit once again.

For a last moment, I hold our embrace. Knowing that this is just. My silver hand
pulling
his yellow hair as my other arm locks his pitiful body against me.

                                        Then, I relent . . .
                                                  drawing
                                        myself from him.
          Leaving him to my curse.

His eyes close . . . the soporific effect of my night-embrace left him in a stupor.

I lay him on his back and the floor ripples around him--slowly swallowing his body
with a silent gulp.

                              And as his face disappears
                              beneath the now-solid metal --

I KNOW
that I have been here alone all along.

I realize that the woman, the man,

the maze itself . . .

are all extensions of me.

At once, six walls slam down around me -- disallowing any further progress.

But The Truth has awakened within me.

I will not be denied . . .

in careful meditation , I remember . . .

that I chose to come here,

that I heard the voice call to my loneliness,

that I punished myself for my misery by witnessing that scene,

that I willed my own death when confronted with my weakness,

that I commanded my redemption here and now   --

All of this has always been mine!

The gray walls shimmer for a moment,

unsure of my thoughts and actions   --

I am in control . . .

as I always was.

So I try to will myself free . . .

but the walls begin to contract around me . . .

tighter   tighter . . .

perhaps there IS someone else here . . .

"Know this . . . A prison that I control remains a prison -- WHEN I escape, it will be your turn."

My words echo, almost mockingly. But I will be deceived no more. The wall before me vanishes as I decide to walk forward. The darkness embraces me at my first stride, providing some comfort.

I have the knowledge, all I require is the opportunity.

*   *   *   *   *

VOICE

4th Lunar Cycle, 2053
Southern Central Rocky Mountains

I am Cochise, leader of this Apache community. My people live simple lives, away
from the pressures and complexity of the outside world.
    But little by little,
        day by day, all of this changes.

Whether it is, Mitchell Walker's opening a grocery,
                    so we <u>don't need</u> to grow our food;
      or   Lisie Runs like Water buys a car
                    so she <u>doesn't have to</u> walk to work;
      or   little Eagle Eyes convincing his parents to buy a computer,
                    so he can escape the world in this valley;
and the chaos creeps deeper in our community's veins.

                              Many of the people don't
                                  see it -- the loss of our
                                traditions, the ignorance
                             of our history, the neglect
                                    of our values.

                    But I do.
          Yet even this vision provides
               no answers.

All I find in my
search for answers is
a blinding light.

     Seventeen days into the cycle, sunlight pours in through my bedroom window
...
     my grandmother once told me that angels walked on those beams of light.

        Today, I know
                my answering angel will arrive.

               .
               .
               .

The cool water felt wonderful as I splashed it against my scalp, running my fingers
   backwards over my head. It took only a half-hour to pull my thick gray braid
   together--after 60 solar revolutions, I still liked the weight and feel of the braid
   on my brown leather jacket.

My face was heavier than it had been . . . 20 SRs ago . . . when I became tribal
leader . . . The wrinkles have grown thicker and multiplied. But my eyes --
the same dark brown with a little sparkle. The darkness might cloak my body,
but it has yet to pierce my soul.

Crisply warm, the air and sun on my cheeks. Yet even my breath tastes the growing
malaise.

The children still played, the women still cooked, the men still hunted -- but there were
changes.

There was more hairpulling, teasing, and fighting;
    more jealousy, competition, and gossip;
    more boasting, cruelty, and murder.
                                        Yet none of them saw.

When Eagle Eyes' little brown hand reached up and pulled on my sleeve, I thought I
would cry when he said, "Mordug, Maula!"
        (Apollyonian translation: "Good morning, father!")

The very words from his mouth were solid, complete sybaritic syllables. My heart
fell to my feet, and the dark chill breathed on my soul.

"Good morning, child." The only action harder than patting the boy's head was
exhaling the words as I looked into the young eyes, which now seemed so old.

He turned and ran off -- even his small, racing steps appeared mechanical,
somehow less natural.

That was just the beginning as silently, surging obsidian swarmed my village.

Quietly, it began.
    The women--my sisters, daughters, and mothers--returned from the fields with
        wheelbarrows filled with metallic, dark foods. They snacked on them as
        they walked, grinding the twisted roots with steel-razor teeth.

    The men--my brothers, sons, and fathers--yelled battlecries and dragged pound
        after carrion pound back to us. Far more meat than we could ever eat. I
        prayed the Apology Prayer to Buffalo for this carnage. They joyously
        licked the crimson from their metal-bladed digits which had done this
        grisly work.

At that moment, they recognized me . . .

"Refnig! Ante daler nyrom!"
("Foreigner! You are our leader -- no more!!")
Tall Mountain's words beat on
me more than his
newly-ferrous arms ever
could.

"Rudetin . . . pprancate nosmashotd."
("Intruder . . . your appearance shames us all.")
Elisabeth's legs sparkled
in the light, yet I knew
they would carry her
no faster.

"Obeng, 'maula' dosapa! Obgen!"
("Begone, past 'teacher'! Begone!")
The children chanted
with one voice,
mocking me,
spiting me,

until my only choice
was
to
flee.

*   *   *

    How the darkness found my people I may never know. But their consumption is my responsibility. It is my fault that they couldn't see the impending fate, that they could not resist this creeping doom.

    Dashing through the forest, twigs and branches lashed out at me --
ripping at my arms, legs, and face. I kept tripping and falling -- raw
scrapes covered my hands and knees. My beautiful leather jacket, my
father's before me, was torn and tattered. Finally, after running for hours,
the horror and fear and bitterness exhausted my reserves and I collapsed
at the foot of a hill -- Spent emotionally, spiritually, and physically.

.
.
.

Haze purple steadied into an orange glow. Blurred edges surrendered to crisp
memory,

repressed no longer.

The nearby river's peaceful lapping soothed with its familiarity, but only momentarily. A small boy swam back and forth playfully as his father looked on from the shore. As they came into focus, the vision became painful.

It was my father sitting there, wearing the jacket I donned earlier. That could only mean that this was the day I had nearly died. Suddenly, my lungs contracted in somatic pain. I trembled at the realization. Reliving this, I could not. Yet forward pushed the scene.

The river flowed darker, rougher, sharper. And my small head disappeared beneath the swelling waves. Father dashed to the river edge, only to be driven back by a wall of solid water.

As a child, I had struggled helplessly to escape the suffocating grasp under the water. In seconds, it had pinned me to the sediment with a strength so concrete … minutes later, the last bubbles floated away from my desperate, collapsed body.

Now, I saw what transpired at the surface – an exchange that changed the course of my life without my knowledge or consent.

My father howled at his impotence as the skies darkened unnaturally. It was a disturbing sound, broken assiduously by a crackling voice from the forest.

"Nioc amevaste." ("You may yet save the boy.")

Father's head snapped to attention, searching for the source of this offer.

Ten meters to his right, tiny, contorted faces – hundreds of them – appeared in the thick trunk of a nearby redwood tree. Fear seized my father's body as he recognized the demonic presence confronting him. This monster would certainly take his son, me, from him without a moment's hesitation. From this situation, there would be no satisfactory conclusion. Evil held him completely.

"Sgnoywse repleote; gritne surste sopssel. Deterowl osbridnosha, rep vulvenos." ("Your people are wise and strong; they possess the integrity to resist us. We shall soon be driven from your world, but we will return stronger.")

"So? What has this to do with my son? Release him! Please …"
My father struggled to utter these words. His body shook violently at the effort.

"Shanos – nsetexche tviclnte ostuna. Senrpso … luveytrog multse. Gotthe, rapadtur totsotiw. Rapt, mbramur niote hroa, pleey, trea." ("We shall -- in exchange for your consent to visit your enclave at our return. Our presence … stimulates evolution and growth. Together, a true paradise awaits us all. Apart, death embraces your son now, and your people, later.")

Hideous grins nearly split the tree in half as the faces reveled in their abuse of a good man and his values.

Torn among ignorance, terror, exasperation, and rage, my father felt his knees buckle and his soul shortly followed.

"Very well … I agree." Kneeling still, his face rose to the demon-tree as he said. "My son, now and alive, as you promised."

Before the last word escaped his throat, the river spat me from its bosom with a quiet belch. My small body was drenched when it landed next to my father. He touched my chest and the thick, clear liquid flowed from my mouth and nose. I inhaled.

Witnessing the scene, I almost wished I could throw myself back into the streaming flow. I now knew the exact cause of my village's transformation. It was my living.

In the vision, my father began to cry. Immediately, he rebelled by whispering in my ear, "Never surrender. Win the battle I could not."

I never remembered this command, but now I heard it through my soul.   I almost felt his arms around me again as the orange evening sky faded to purple, and the vision ended.

Could I summon the strength I needed now?
*   *   *

Again, the warm light flooded through my eyelids . . . breaking the doubting urgency ringing in my mind. I almost thought I was home again . . . but before I could even open my eyes, reality checked me.

"The darkness has not yet broken you. I shall return you to your home--fuller than you left."

This voice which addressed me so confidently, seemed little more than a whisper, yet it
> reverberated in my mind. It seems to clear away the blighted edges of my perceptions and open my mind Truly for the first time in years.

As I raised my eyelids, pain shot through my eyes -- the Sun itself stood before me!! Scurrying backwards up the hill, I hid my face in my hands and tried to rub away the pain.

"It will hurt some but only for a moment."

Soothing, like a warm bath . . . this voice. I paused in my retreat and tumbled back to the foot of the hill.

A deep burning sensation in my left leg made my cry out -- but it didn't really hurt. Somehow . . . as the feeling tingled up my left side to the crown of my head, then back down my side . . . it felt right -- this burning.

When it left my right foot, I began to cough and hack at something in my throat . . . tears poured from the corners of my eyes, my body trembled with the effort, and saliva ran down my chin, but, finally, it was dislodged and flew out of my mouth.

An ebony stone. It hit the ground for a moment and began to roll back towards me. A blue line appeared with a 'zing', striking the rock. And it vanished.

The voice.

I turn slowly, keeping my eyes to the ground . . . his feet glow bright yellow, as do his legs. His whole body shines solid gold -- his eyes meet mine squarely and I know I am in the presence of Father Sky. My head drops in despair . . .

"Forgive me--I have failed you and my people. They are overcome by the darkness. I am at your mercy!"

A warm finger touched my forehead, making my gaze meet his again.

"Then, we have some work to do."

His touch blended our perceptions, he saw what I knew and I knew what he planned.

Strength filled my limbs as I rose to my feet. Feeling better than I had in months, I showed Father Sky the way with purpose and confidence. His power gave me hope again.

*   *   *

In just hours, the village had been transformed. Dark storm clouds gathered ominously overhead and thunder exploded without lightning. Animal heads were spiked on posts and torches burned with black-flame, casting silvery light eerily over everything. The paths were empty, and a distant humming was the only sound to be heard.

Then, as I reached the center of the village, the source of the sound stood revealed. The travesty nearly forced me to flee again -- but Father Sky's hand grasped

mine and steadied me.
They -- my people had caked themselves in tar and danced the Ghost Dance
backwards around a huge onyx bonfire. A platinum face shone in the midst of it, but
was partially obscured. It was . . . male, but something hung from his left eye . . .

My observation was interrupted as some of the women noticed us. Four
charged forward, naked and shrieking -- 3 silver and 3 black tentacles had replaced
each of their arms and they whipped at us wildly.

Father Sky stood his ground and raised both hands towards them -- the swirling,
prismatic glow formed an orb around each hand before four bolts streaked into the
women's bodies. Their howls stopped the perverted dance and the entire village turned
-- just in time to see the bodies fall-alive, but all traces of the darkness eliminated.

Enraged--the entire village swarmed over the bodies, re-establishing their
misshapen darkforms almost instantly.

"Vagnoste lasido, ty bbrakite Wakata-gu? Hoa tetob motre!"
      ("We let you go, and you return with the Lightbringer? Now you both will die!")

Leaping, charging, running over each other to get to us, my people's transformation
      looked complete. Father Sky raised a golden wall between us and them. But
      with a thunderous blow, Tall Mountain destroyed the barrier. Tendrils from the
      mob wrapped around Father Sky's arms and dragged him to the floor.
      Exploding
      upwards, he escaped, but his blasts of light were no longer undoing the
      transformations.
            Then, I heard Eagle Eyes,
                              "Vetekab, maula . . ."
      ("Watch your back, Father . . .")   his malicious laughter followed.

            His claw ripped across my back, and I fell forward. Father Sky battled
      valiantly, but his efforts only slowed the dark progression. I roll onto my back
      and face young Eagle eyes -- his stare bloodthirsty, emotionless. My blood
      dripped from his right razorfingertips into small red puddles on the ground. The
      image reminded me of a chant I learned when I was his age. And, in my
      reminiscence, the chant grew louder in my mind until it poured forth from my
      throat.

Eagle Eyes raised his hand   to disembowel me ,
            but, at the last moment, he heard my song . . .

                                                      "Hey, yunga . . .
                                                      Ho -- yunga . . .
                                                      Hey, yung-yung"

Mantric repetition seized my voice, and slowly a light sparked behind Eagle Eyes'
pupils. His soul heard me.
If only everyone
could hear,
maybe . . .

Father Sky had never broken our link, he felt my wish and made it true. Eagle Eyes
began to mouth,   the words.
then sing,   His body came to look more like a little boy's --
as jet ink flowed from his eyes and ears --
and gradually, the body was his again.

He helped me up with a smile I had not seen in many LCs.   We sang together.

"Hey--Yunga,   Ho-Yunga,   He-ey-yung-yung . . ."

Slowly, the fringes of the group attacking Father Sky heard us and the light flared in
them. It began to slowly re-balance them. Their voices then joined ours.

For the first time in years, the community acted with purpose as a unit. And the
less they acted against Father Sky, the more their voices healed them. Soon, our
entire village's mighty voice coalesced as a golden wave of light which Father Sky
absorbed, then expelled in all directions.

The blast swept the excess darkness from our valley, cracked the black cloud-
ceiling which denied us the sun. The vegetables were recast healthy, and the extra
deer and buffalo sprung back to life.

For less than a minute, twin suns glowed in our sky. Then, Father Sky landed next to
me, gripping my hand, and said, "Father Sky only sent me, I am Danzuro ... the
Lightbringer. Soon, all the world shall follow your example. Thank you. Thank
you so much for rekindling the Light here."

Pointing to my chest, I said, "Thank YOU for rekindling the Light here. And you
ARE
Father Sky, good luck in freeing Mother Earth." With purpose, I squeezed
his
hand and I saw him feel the warmth of love flowing from me.

Streaking to the horizon, he vanished in a flash. But his heart trail joins our chant,
as our village prepared a celebratory feast.

*   *   *   *   *

FULL CIRCLE

Ninth Lunar Cycle, 2054
SanFranland, North America

I don't know how long I've been wandering in this, my maze.
        It seems, like, ...must have been... months
                Maybe years...
Maybe moments.

        Time holds no substance for me.
        Place abdicates all meaning here.

Each corridor is a simple variation of the last...
        Straight ten paces, turn left.
        Straight fives paces, turn right.
        Straight ten paces, turn right.
        Straight five paces, turn left.

And so on *ad nauseum*, were I capable of nausea.

I have taken command here - still it has been so
                                                                long.

        I must not   will not
                                                forget.

I eternally ... unceasingly ... move forward ...
        step
                        after
                                        step
                                                after
                                                        step

Incapable of exhaustion, I give credit to someone who, I hope, created this perfect
prison. This holding cell I can control, but never escape.

I hope that someone else built this, so that the idea of revenge will keep me
                                                        sane.
                        "Unque terlat."
                ("What a relative term.")

I stop and I ...
                I hear a chuckle.

"WHO SAID THAT!?!"

I lash out with my platinum form in all directions--reshaping the walls, yet finding no source – I am evaded with ridiculous ease.

"WHO SAID THAT!?!" I hiss as I collapse to the floor.

Slowly, I feel the floor creep up between my fingers ...
                                                    covering ...
                    spreading ... over my hands before
                                          I
                                          could
                                          pull away!

In the next instant, the dark metallic floor had coated my torso and the fronts of my legs.

            Sealed to the floor, I sense the ceiling and walls as they contract around me.

                  I was completely covered by the former maze's substance with
                            the speed of thought.

A slight humanoid frame appears in the peripheral shadows of my perception.

Then,
            my eyelids slammed shut
            under the weight of their
            metallic shells.
            *   *   *
Finally,
            too long delayed my arrival has been.
Hordes of darkspawn unsuccessfully resisted my progress.
Their efforts stand insufficient.

Here I stand.
SanFranland.

It's decimated ... a mere shadow of its former glory.
            Burnt out skyscrapers, streets ripped into mountains
                                    of concrete and asphalt by the tectonic shifts
caused by the Disunion of the Ka.
            Automobiles crumbled, flipped,
                                    some on fire.
            Huddled humanoid figures scuffle through the shadows,
                  averting their eyes from my brilliance as I float pass them.

Neon signs periodically shatter on the street in small explosions,

    I absorb the resulting energy; I will
            need it in the coming conflict.

Since 'touching' Rosha at Zodar's birth, I have
    followed her spirit-trail here. Her incarceration
    ends today.

I turn a corner and am amazed ...

   This street is a virtual mountain range of deconstructed
                   modernity.
    A slab of asphalt cleaves the air to a height of 10 meters,
        and several others reach just shorter.
Wreckage is everywhere, and I begin to float up ...
        to negotiate my way most easily.

A long chain lashes out at me from one of the buildings.
      I grab one end and pull.
    A youth flies forth from a window, holding the other end.
I throw the chain and the child into an adjacent building.
    I sense his wounds and feel him fade into
                      unconsciousness.

"Sseparet!!" ("Trespasser!!")
  Gangs of children, malnourished and gaunt, scramble out
     from
     the
     debris.

     Throwing anything they can lift, they provide
                little danger
                to me.
    I continue on my way, increasing my heat output to incinerate their projectiles.

"UV! Unque sobc klatp brose!" ("Hey! That's the one the boss was talking about!")

The Boss?!?
I turn to face the voice.
    A Gatling gun fires round after round of high-velocity metal at me.

Again, I raise my external temperature ...
this time, to 20 degrees Kelvin--exploding the
bullets in mid-flight.
Adjusting the frequency and wavelength of my solid-photon
form, I render my body invisible.
After melting the machine gun to slag, I begin to feel

a distinct change   (colder)
in the climate around me.

The source of this energy matrix convenes around an older child who waves her
arms, dropping the temperature around me to freezing--trying to make me vulnerable.

With a thought, dazzling light streaks from my raised hands,
striking the child,
smiting her senseless temporarily.

The children begin to struggle over each other to get away and hide.
Bending into a laser, I teleport in front of one of them.

He falls to his knees, hiding his face in his hands.
He cannot have seen more than 6 Earth orbits.

The look in his eyes, as I raise his head,
reminds me ... of the boy I saw ...
when I first awoke ...
the boy I killed ...

I shudder at the power karmic.

And my eyes lock on his and I send a portion of my essence into his soul through
those   mystical windows.

The child is filled with radiant
contagious
hope.
He smiles, for perhaps the first time.
I learn Rosha's whereabouts from our communion.

I rise to take my leave.
As I look over my shoulder, I see the child,
running
touching
hugging
kissing

spreading
his Midas touch
of golden Hope to all of the others.

The Ka will be reunited.
These children will know a "Boss" no more.

*   *   *

The metal casings lift from my eyes, and I open them.
My body trembles slightly under the weight of the
metal encasing me.

A mechanism approaches me ... Even through my shell, I can hear the servo motors
driving its legs.

Its approach is slow, almost uncoordinated.
The maker is amazingly advanced, as I can feel by
my prison,

Why is this creation so sloppy?
I strain my eyes to see its face ...
and immediately wish I hadn't.

its wild white hair points in all directions
its mouth hangs open with strings of saliva falling out
its left eye dangles precariously by its retinal cord
halfway down his face

"Vete pprecta ypprecna," it gargles.
("I see you appreciate my appearance.")

"He. Kapeste init nlukcy tomte."
("Oh, yes. You can't speak until I unlock your mouth.")
<HA-HA-HA-HA, tee-hee, tee-hee, tee-hee>

I find his utter insanity
familiar,   almost
appealing ...

His chaotic being makes him almost a sibling.

"REO TQIAN"

("BUT NOT QUITE")

He knows my thoughts!

"TQI TERV"
("QUITE TRUE")

Stop screaming!

"ANANANANANANANANANANANANAN!!!," he shrieks.
("NOOOOOOOOOOOOOOOOOOOOOOO!!!")

"I'll converse in your silly tongue for awhile."
"You knew you weren't unique, didn't you?"
"Well, you're not. It's true. Ironically, I was born the moment that you and Danzuro met. And all that the Ka sought to deny …

pain	greed	envy
lust	violence	fear
sloth	betrayal	evil

these reshaped me -- mere moments before my birth and their elimination -- in the hope that I could destroy the Ka.   I am Chaos reborn."

Keep my mind blank.

"Yes!! Do shut up for awhile! I've been listening to you complain and whine in my maze for months now! Anyway ... When I was born--a twisted mechanical mockery of a human child--my mother died of shock, and, in my rage, I used my metallic appendages to kill the incompetents who could not save her. It was only a matter of time before I used my ability to manipulate metals and machines, combined with the evil within me, to generate the Darkness-Well which pulled you from the Ka.   My creation destroyed the Ka and trapped you in my never-ending Metal-Maze. However, the energy discharge from the separation his Danzuro from me for a time. Your Dark essence served me well in the transformation of this world and the creation of DarkSpawn to lure the Lightbringer here.
Where I can destroy him myself!!"
<HA-HA, tee-hee>

Does he ever shut up?

"NO! But the best part is that even though Danzuro may temporarily convert some away from the Dark, when he comes to rescue you, I'll use your sweet, chaotic substance to destroy him."

And, with him, any hope of restoring the Ka!"
<HA-HA-HA-HA-HA,
HA-HA-HA-HA-HA>

*   *   *

The lighted wire fences mark the borders of a glittering tower of technology. I sense Rosha's presence inside this pulsing, silently foreboding, postmodern marvel.

I modulate my body's frequency to render myself invisible, and I release the majority of my protons to lower my density to virtually nothing.

Invisible and intangible, I enter the central tower with ease.

.

.

.

The guard at the front desk continues his normal activity
as I enter the elevator shaft.

I float up
        and
  up
        and
  up
  Until I arrive at the 49th floor.

My senses guided me here, but there is only another elevator door.

Wary,
I attempt to step through the doors,
only to be rebuffed and knocked to the floor.

So densely packed are the molecules in the elevator doors,
that even my ghostly body finds access forbidden.

The doors slide open --
an invitation.
I will not turn back.

Regaining my tangibility, I enter ...

<WHOOOOSH!!>

It is an express-elevator, and I am lifted higher from the floor
due to its speed.

It glides to a stop, and the doors slide open.

<Bratta-tat-tat, Bratta-tat-tat>

I respond to the gunfire by instinctively raising the ambient air temperature in front of me,
expecting to incinerate the bullets ...

Too late I see they are Dark substance, and they sail right through ...
invading my luminous form.

I howl in agony and throw a multispectrum photon burst forward
through the open elevator doors, hoping
to burn whatever shot me to a crisp!

For a long moment, there is silence.
I prop myself against the back wall of the
elevator, lifting myself slowly.

<Bratta-tat-tat, Bratta-tat-tat>

I fall face forward, feeling the Dark substance creeping
through me, corrupting the Light, and trying to free
the Darkness within me.
In my mind, I hear my core cry out
"Necho"
("Night")
And again, I howl--
this time in fear,

.

.

.

Focusing again on my attackers, I
allow my photons to commingle with the atoms of
the elevator floor.
I then spread my substance in the floor of the lab in
front of me.
I perceive that the agents before me are carrying
reflective shields. That explains how they avoided my
multispectrum blast.
They are corrupted humans   —   Darkspawn.
I know how to defeat them.

They emerge from their protected positions to check on me in the elevator, not

bothering to look at the floor beneath them. They step on to my expanding form ...
      the first two,
            (Necho)thepoundinginmyheadisgettinglouder
                  the next two
            (Necho)andmore(Necho)frequent(Necho)

                                          the last two ... ,
            (Necho)   (Necho)
                  I have them.

I flood them, their bodies, with my being. I share (Necho) with them my experience
of love, joy, hope, and (Necho) peace, overwhelming their experiences (Necho) of
pain, ignorance, anger, and jealousy.
      One by one, they (Necho) drop to the floor unconscious and cleansed.

I sense (Necho) a room hidden behind the (Necho) south wall,
      I melt it open (Necho) from a distance ...

There is a metallic sculpture of Rosha kneeling in a spotlight.
      I struggle (Necho) forward (Necho) quickly to (Necho)
      examine it.

(Necho) Just as I pass the portal, another door seals off
                                          my retreat. (Necho)
            The sculpture's head (Necho) turns to me.
            (Necho) Its eyes . . . (Necho)

(Necho)(Necho)   IT'S HER!!   (Necho)(Necho)

                              "HA-HA-HA-HA-HA!!!!"

Immediately, Darkforce floods the room, swallowing me whole.
            (Necho)(Necho)(Necho)(Necho)(Necho)(Necho)(Necho)
            (Necho)(Necho)(Necho)(Necho)(Necho)(Necho)(Necho)

My Black core breaks free, I am overwhelmed . . .
                                          I collapse to the ceiling.
The world is done.
                  I have failed.

*   *   *

it has made a mistake.
   I reach out to the Blackness he has summoned against Danzuro,
         marshalling its strength,
            directing its force ...
I crush my metal prison through a combination of

                    implosion and explosion.

            This fate awaits its maker as well.

I rejoice in my freedom and revel in my Darkness.
I feel the creature scrambling to a sewer grate in a futile attempt
                                                at escape.

I slam the grate shut and seal it with a Black cover as I cross the room.

                                        He looks at me over his shoulder.
                        In his eyes, the approach of a chrome angel
                                    followed by an ebony maelstrom
                                                    is reflected.

                    I skewer him against the wall with a silver stalagmite.
            With Black tentacles, I rip the mechanical limbs from him,
                        leaving only a sorry, never-human torso.

He screams, "Death is but a stage between lives, I shall return!"
I reply, "Come, then. I shall be waiting."

My Darkness seeps from the piercing spear into, and all over, his body. His
misshapen head I consume slowly, at last.

        Then, the shadowy form crumbles, utterly expunged -- the dark shards
vanish into the shadows at the intersection of the floor and wall.

                                        .

                                        .

                                        .

    Rosha turns back to Danzuro.
    His right hand plants on the floor as he struggles to rise, his glow just
        returning.
    Touching his chest and drawing out the excess Darkness, she asks, "You ok?"

    "For having stared death in the eye?" Brilliance drips from his smile. "Quite well,
thank you."

        They exchange snide, sidelong looks.

"Then I suggest we get to business."
                                Rosha extends her hand as she speaks.

"Yes, it is time."

At the first joining of these primal opposites, an energy ripple spread forth, changing the fabric of reality as it proceeded.
This time, as Danzuro places his hand in hers, the ripple of transformation extends inwards.

And just as the Ka approaches rebirth, the miracle is
halted.   Slowly, Rosha and Danzuro realize there is still one
piece missing.

Zodar.

*   *   *

With the spontaneity of instinct, the neo-nascent, still dual Ka is in the Canadian Shield Region.

Danzuro guided them to the mountain he left, but in its place, there is only
a small patch of green grass . . . and worse yet .
. .

No Zodar!!

"Impossible! I left him right here!"

Danzuro's shock meets Rosha's inquiring gaze.

She vaguely remembers touching a place like this. It comforted her during a dream while she was imprisoned ... but where is the child she saw there?

"Where are you?" she whispers.

"I am here." The voice came from the air and the ground and somewhere else. Rosha and Danzuro both recognize it as the child's.

"The Ka disintegrated because it was unity representing multiplicity, presence representing absence. When you created me, I was an amalgamation of the two of you. As I grew, I knew I must become the multiplicity, the absence you lacked. Now we all are ready."

The child's wisdom sparked the moment of the Ka's rebirth. Rosha and Danzuro stood together for a instant, then embraced. Then, Zodar blended the two of them into one.

Reflective platinum raced into luminescent Gold as they began to rotate,
then spiral,
then spin
together, a meter above the ground.

Their merged form slid to the ground, and once again, the ripple effect swept over the Earth.

*   *   *   *   *

The new Ka gave itself so that all reality might exist in balance. Forever more, all that exists and doesn't exist will have something of the Ka. It is, was, and will be a force and a non-force.

It is -- in everything -- the unpredictable, asymmetrical beauty of being and non-being which is damned and divine, and which exists between and beyond the two. It manifests in life, death, earth, air, water, fire, plants, animals, and each and every one of us.

This was the Life of the Ka as recorded by the Griot.

Printed in the United States
72965LV00001B/343-440

9 781425 956